Going thr  Galatians

With Michael Penny

A Study Guide to Paul's First Letter

ISBN: 978-1-78364-542-8

www.obt.org.uk

****

The Open Bible Trust
Fordland Mount, Upper Basildon,
Reading, RG8 8LU, UK.

Going through Galatians

with
Michael Penny

Introduction

This series of studies is designed to be used either for personal study and meditation or for group discussion.

After the initial study, giving the background to Paul's letter to the Galatians, further studies are in two parts.

- First there are questions which bring out the interpretation in its historical context.
- Then there are questions seeking applications to 21st Century society.

I hope you will enjoy this series on Galatians and will learn a lot about this first letter written by the Apostle Paul. However, it may help at times to refer to my book *Galatians: Interpretation and Application*, which first puts the historical setting (the interpretation) of each passage, before dealing with various applications for today.

Details of this book can be seen on www.obt.org.uk

It can be ordered from that website but …

It is available as an eBook from Amazon and Apple and as a paperback from Amazon.

Going through Galatians

with Michael Penny

Study 1

The Background to Galatians

The Background to Galatians

People

When reading the New Testament, we should be aware of five different types of people.

1. The Jews:

These are descendants of Abraham through Isaac and Jacob, and were members of one of the Twelve Tribes (Acts 26:7; James 1:1).

2. Proselytes:

In some Bibles this technical term is translated 'converts to Judaism', which is exactly what they were. These were Gentiles who kept the Sabbath and had been circumcised. They were welcomed into the Jewish nation, could participate in synagogue worship, and enter the inner courts of the Jerusalem temple to offer sacrifices etc. (Isaiah 56:6-7).

3. God fearers:

One aspect of the Assyrian and Babylonian conquest

was to exile Israel and 'disperse' the Jews throughout their empires.

Even though the Medo-Persians allowed them to return and rebuild Jerusalem and the temple, many did not: they remained where they were and became known as the *diaspora:* the dispersion or the scattered (see James 1:1; 1 Peter 1:1).

In their cities and towns, they built synagogues and a number of Gentiles, who had become disillusioned with the worship of such pagan deities as Zeus or Bacchus, started to attend the synagogues.

They could not participate in the worship and usually sat behind a screen or to the side or upstairs. And if they went up to Jerusalem they could only enter the outer courts of the temple.

In time, some of them chose to be circumcised and become Proselytes: some did not.

There were many of these God fearers at the time and the two most notable ones in the New Testament are a centurion, who built a synagogue in Capernaum, and Cornelius, the first Gentile Peter visited (Luke 7:1-10; Acts 10:1-2).

4. Pagans:

This term is wide and covers the educated philosophers in Athens as well as the uneducated dockers in Corinth, and everyone in between.

5. The Judaisers

These are also referred to as 'the circumcision group' or 'the circumcision party'; (Galatians 2:12; Titus 1:10). These were a group of Christian Jews who did not fully understand the gospel of salvation by grace through faith.

They taught it was 'necessary' to believe in Christ but it was not 'sufficient'; people had also to be circumcised (Acts 15:1-2). These are called believers in Acts 15:5.

Jerusalem

Before Barnabas and Paul set off on their first missionary journey, which eventually took them into Galatia, they went up to Jerusalem.

Q1: What prompted them to go to Jerusalem? (See Acts 11:27-30)

Q2: What happened in Jerusalem? (See Galatians 2:1-10)

They then returned to Antioch in Syria.

Q3. What happened then in Antioch? (See Acts 12:27 – 13:1-4)

Q4: Why did Barnabas and Paul go first to Cyprus? (See Acts 4:36; 11:19-20)

First Missionary Journey

The places visited on that first missionary journey can be seen on the map on the next page, and the details of what happened can be read in the passages below.

Cyprus – Acts 13:4-12
    Salamis – Acts 13:5
    Paphos – Acts 13:6-12

Region of Galatia – Acts13:13 – 14:25
    Antioch in Pisidia – 13:13-51

Iconium – Acts 13:51-14:6
Lystra – 14:6-20
Derbe – 14:20-21
Lystra, Iconium, Antioch and region of Pisidia –
14:21-24

Region of Pamphylia – Acts 14:24-25
Perga and Attalia – Acts 14:25

Back to Antioch in Syria – Acts 14:26-28

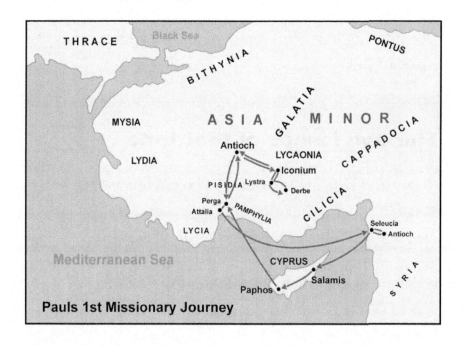

Pauls 1st Missionary Journey

Note: Acts 14:28: They were there, at Antioch in Syria, a long time!

> Q5: What happened when they were there? (Galatians 2:1-10; Acts 15:1-2)

What happened in Antioch was also happening in Galatia, which was why Paul wrote the letter. He may have wanted to return to Galatia immediately, but he could not.

> Q6: Why couldn't Paul return to Galatia immediately? (Acts 15:2-3)

The two issues of that time

Primarily: Did Gentiles have to be circumcised to be saved?
Secondarily: Did they have to keep the Law of Moses?

Galatians was written to deal with these issues.

Circumcision:
There are 13 references to 'circumcision' in Galatians: see 2:3; 2:7-9; 2:12; 5:2-3; 5:6; 5:11; 6:12-13; 6:15. (See pages 16-21 of *Galatians: Interpretation and Application* which deals with these in detail.)

The Law of Moses

There are 27 references to the 'law': see

2:16,19,21;

3:1,3,5,10-13,15,17-19,21,23,24;

4:4,5,21;

5:3,4; 5:14,18,23

(These passages are also dealt with in *Galatians: Interpretation and Application.*)

As mentioned above, Paul wrote Galatians to deal with circumcision and Law keeping, but the letter also has other corrective teaching as well as words of encouragement.

It was written to a 'group' of churches and, as such, contains little personal comment about individuals.

The Letter to the Galatians

As this letter was written before the Jerusalem Council of Acts 15:16-21 Paul could not use its decision to support his teaching. Please read Galatians and ask:

Q7: How good were Paul's arguments against the two issues?

Q8: Do you think he was successful?

Going through Galatians

with Michael Penny

Study 2:
Galatians 1:1-10

Defending the Gospel

Galatians 1:1-5

1. What is an apostle?
2. Name 4 churches in Galatia. (Acts 13:13-14:23)
3. Define grace.
4. Define peace.
5. Why did Paul call the time when he was living an "evil age"?
6. What did Paul say is "according to the will of our God and Father"?

Galatians 1:6-10

7. What was it that astonished Paul?

8. What was this "different gospel"?

9. What was the "gospel of Christ"?

10. How was the "gospel of Christ" being perverted?

11. Which gospel did Paul preach?

12. Why was this "different gospel" no gospel at all?

13. What was the effect of this "different gospel" upon the Galatian Christians?

14. What was Paul's reaction towards those who preached a different gospel?

15. Do you think Paul's attitude towards these Judaisers, who were Christians, was extreme?

16. These Judaisers, those who preached a "different gospel", which men were they pleasing?

17. Did Paul try to please these men?

Application

1. Would we describe today as "an evil age"?
2. What is the true gospel for our dispensation?
3. Circumcision is not an issue for Christians today, but what other things have been added to "the gospel of Christ"?
4. What should be our attitude towards those who add to "the gospel of Christ"?
5. What sort of things, today, have been "taken" from the gospel of Christ?
6. Is "adding" to the gospel of Christ better or worse than (or just as bad as) "taking" from the gospel of Christ?

Going through Galatians

with Michael Penny

Study 3:
Galatians 1:11-24

Problems for Paul

Galatians 1:11-24

1. What was the origin of Paul's gospel?
2. What was Paul's gospel?
3. In what ways had Paul persecuted the church?
4. What achievements had Paul gained before he was a Christian? (See also Philippians 3:4-6.)
5. For what purpose was Paul saved? (See also Acts 9:15-16; is there any contradiction here with Galatians 1:16 and Galatians 2:9?)
6. Paul went from Damascus, to Arabia, and then back to Damascus: see map opposite. What did he do in Damascus and Arabia, part of which was in the Nabataean Kingdom? (See Acts 9:19-26; 2 Corinthians 11:32-33; Aretas was King of the Nabataeans.)
7. Is there a contradiction between Galatians 1:17-18 and Acts 9:19-26?
8. Which Apostles did Paul see in Jerusalem? (See also Acts 9:26-28.)
9. Why did Saul go to Syria and Cilicia? (See Acts 9:28-30.)
10. What was the reaction of the churches in Judea?
11. How many churches were there in Judea, when were they started and who had started them?
12. How long was Paul in Tarsus (Syria and Cilicia; see map on the next page) and what did he do there for all that time? (See Galatians 2:1; we are talking about 11 or 14 years.)

Application

1. From whom did we learn the gospel?
2. What were our achievements in the world before we were Christians?
3. What are our achievements in the world, outside of Christianity, and what value are these? (See Philippians 3:7-9, but be careful to read it accurately.)
4. For what purpose(s) were we saved? (See Ephesians 2:10.)
5. Who do we consult?
6. What is the general report about us?
7. Have we had fallow periods in our Christian life?

Going through Galatians

with Michael Penny

Study 4:
Galatians 2:1-10

The Meeting in Jerusalem

Galatians 2:1-10

1. "Fourteen years later". Is that 14 years after his previous visit or 14 years after his conversion?
2. Either way, Paul was a long time away from the action in Jerusalem and Judea: where was he, and what did he do?
3. Who went with Paul to Jerusalem?
4. Why did they go?
5. What did he do there?
6. Why does he mention that Titus was not compelled to be circumcised by the Jewish Christian leaders?
7. To whom is Paul referring to in verses 4 & 5?
8. To what is he referring to in verses 4 & 5?
9. Is Paul being off-handed, sarcastic, or derogatory in any way towards those who are important (the leaders)? (See v 6.)
10. What did these leaders conclude?
11. An apostle means 'a sent one'. Where, or to whom, was Peter sent?
12. Where, or to whom, was Paul sent?
13. Who else, other than Paul, is called an "Apostle to the *Gentiles*"?
14. Who were the leaders, the important people, the pillars, that Paul met in Jerusalem?
15. How did they react towards Paul and Barnabas?

16. If they agreed for Paul to go to the Gentiles, why did Paul, on his missionary journeys, always go first to the synagogue of the Jews?

17. Did Paul and Barnabas remember the poor on their journeys?

18. What did they do to remember the poor?

Application

1. Have we had long periods of inactivity?
2. Have we ever been pressurised (or do we pressurise others) to conform to certain ceremonies?
3. What sort of 'things' should we persuade people about?
4. How should we treat those in senior positions in the church, even if we disagree with them?
5. Do we remember the poor?

Going through Galatians

with Michael Penny

Study 5:
Galatians 2:11-21

Problems with Peter

Galatians 2:11-21

1. When had Peter been in Antioch?
2. What had Peter done wrong there?
3. Why had Peter done this?
4. What was the effect on others of Peter's action?
5. Why was Peter, really, without excuse? (See Acts 10 and note Acts 11:1-18.)
6. What does Paul mean when he says to Peter, "You are a Jew, yet you live like a Gentile and not like a Jew"?
7. Is Paul talking about Peter not living according to the 'Law' of Moses? Or is he talking about Peter not living according to Jewish 'Customs'? (For more on the difference between the Mosaic LAW and the Jewish CUSTOMS, and Christ's attitude to these, see pages 157-162 of *40 Problem Passages*—passage 22—by Michael Penny.)
8. How are people justified; i.e. made righteous?
9. Compare Galatians 2:16 with Ephesians 2:8-10. Are there any other passages which say similar things?
10. Should followers of Christ be sinless? Can they be, in this life?
11. Should followers of Christ have a lax attitude to sin? (Compare Romans 6:1-2,6)
12. What is Paul referring to in verse 18?
13. How many ways are there of obtaining God's righteousness? And what are they?

Application

1. Do we, or have we, ever opposed fellow-Christians to their face?
2. What was the issue?
3. Have we ever given in to peer pressure and done what we should not have, or not done what we should have?
4. Have we considered the effect our actions (good or bad) have upon other Christians?
5. What are the 'customs' of our church?
6. Do any impinge, even undermine, the gospel of salvation by grace through faith in Christ?
7. Do any impinge upon which other Christians we should fellowship with?

******

This is a difficult section and you may want to read the commentary on these verses in *Galatians: Interpretation and Application* by Michael Penny, and section referred to from the book *40 Problem Passages*.

Details of these book can be seen on www.obt.org.uk

They can be ordered from that website but …

They are available as eBooks from Amazon and Apple and as a paperback from Amazon.

Going through Galatians

with Michael Penny

Study 6:
Galatians 3:1-14

Faith or Observance of the Mosaic Law?

Galatians 3:1-14

1. Who portrayed Jesus Christ crucified before the eyes of the Galatians?

2. Paul's question in verse 2 is critical: Had the Galatians received the Holy Spirit by believing? Or by observance of the Mosaic Law? (Remember faith, belief, trust are three English words which translate basically one Greek word, *pistis*.)

3. Remember, that during the Acts dispensation the Holy Spirit was given with overt / external manifestation of His presence: e.g. Cornelius and household in Acts 10:38-46. Had Cornelius and company received the Spirit by believing what Peter said, or by the observance of the Mosaic Law?

4. Was the Galatians experience similar to that of Cornelius and company?

5. Again, remember that during the Acts dispensation, the Holy Spirit gave each believer a special gift; e.g. 1 Corinthians 12:1-11,27-38. Had they received these gifts by believing in Christ or by observing the Law of Moses?

6. Was the experience in the Galatian churches similar to that in Corinth? (Galatians 3:5)

7. How was Abraham made righteous? (See Romans 4.)
 (a) Was it by observing the Mosaic Law?
 (b) Was it by circumcision?

8. How are the Gentiles justified (made righteous)?

9. It was right and proper for the Christian Jews of the Acts Period to keep and observe the Law of Moses; if they did not, the non-Christian Jews would never have listened to them about Jesus. Thus what does Paul mean by "All who rely on observing the Law are under a curse?

10. Was it 'theoretically' possible to be saved / made righteous by observing the Law?

11. Was it 'practically' possible to be made righteous by observing the Law?

12. What would have been the attitude of any who achieved salvation by the observance of the Law? (Compare Ephesians 2:8-10.)

13. Paul wrote in Romans 7:12 that the Law (and commandments) is holy. Therefore, what was the 'curse of the Law'?

14. How did Christ redeem people from 'the curse of the law'?

15. So, to return to the main theme, why did the Galatians receive the Spirit?

Application

1. Who preached Christ to us? Who explained the Gospel to us? Who sowed the seed that germinated into salvation?
2. Were we saved by observing our church's rituals and regulations?
3. What rituals, today, could be a stumbling block (like circumcision)?
4. Which regulations, today, could be a stumbling block (like the Law of Moses)?

Going through Galatians

with Michael Penny

Study 7:
Galatians 3:15-18

The Law and The Promise:

Part 1

Galatians 3:15-18

1. What does 'duly established' mean?
2. Why couldn't a person add to or set aside or change a covenant (or a will)?
3. When was the promise given to Abraham?
4. When was the Law given to Moses?
5. Which is better? Something established by law or something promised?

The Seed (singular) and Seed (plural) or Seeds

Genesis 17:7-8 *KJV*	Genesis 17:7-8 *NIV*
And I will establish my covenant between me and thee and thy seed after thee in their generations for an everlasting covenant, to be a God unto thee, and to thy seed after thee. And I will give unto thee, and to thy seed after thee, the land wherein thou art a stranger, all the land of Canaan, for an everlasting possession; and I will be their God.	I will establish my covenant as an everlasting covenant between me and you and your descendants after you for the generations to come, to be your God and the God of your descendants after you. The whole land of Canaan, where you are now an alien, I will give as an everlasting possession to you and your descendants after you; and I will be their God.

Note 1: In Genesis 17:7-8, 'seed' is singular, but it refers to Abraham's descendants.

Genesis 21:12 *KJV*	Genesis 21:12 *NIV*
And God said unto Abraham, Let it not be grievous in thy sight because of the lad, and because of thy bondwoman; in all that Sarah hath said unto thee, hearken unto her voice; for in Isaac shall thy seed be called.	But God said to him, "Do not be so distressed about the boy and your maidservant. Listen to whatever Sarah tells you, because it is through Isaac that your offspring will be reckoned."

Note 2: In Genesis 21:12 'seed' is again singular, but this probably refers to the 'promised' seed; i.e. Christ.

Genesis 26:3-4 KJV

Sojourn in this land, and I will be with thee, and will bless thee; for unto thee, and unto thy seed, I will give all these countries, and I will perform the oath which I swore unto Abraham thy father; And I will make thy seed to multiply as the stars of heaven, and will give unto thy seed all these countries; and in thy seed shall all the nations of the earth be blessed.

6. Does 'seed' here refer to Abraham's descendent (plural) or Christ (the promised seed – singular)?

> **Genesis 28:13-14 KJV**
> And, behold, the Lord stood above it, and said, I am the Lord God of Abraham thy father, and the God of Isaac: the land whereon thou liest, to thee will I give it, and to thy *seed;* And thy *seed* shall be as the dust of the earth, and thou shalt spread abroad to the west, and to the east, and to the north, and to the south: and in thee and in thy seed shall all the families of the earth be blessed.

7. Does 'seed' here refer to Abraham's descendent (plural) or Christ (the promised seed – singular)?

> **Hebrews 2:10-11:**
> In bringing many sons to glory, it was fitting that God, for whom and through whom everything exists, should make the author of their salvation perfect through suffering. Both the one who makes men holy and those who are made holy are of the same family. So Jesus is not ashamed to call them brothers.

8. What is the relationship here between the seed (singular) i.e. Christ, and the seed (plural) i.e. the Jews?
9. In Galatians 2:15-18 to which promise or promises is Paul referring?
10. Is Paul saying that the promises made to the seed (plural) have now been transferred to the seed (singular)?
11. Would such a situation be possible under law?

12. Would such a situation be possible under promise; i.e. grace? (Note Romans 4:16).

Application

1. Can we, today, change, add to, or revoke a will?
2. Can we, today, change, add to, or revoke a contract made with another?
3. Today is something established by law better than something promised?
4. Which is better, law or love? (Galatians 5:22-23)
5. What are the political implications today of the promises given to Abraham in Genesis 17:7-8; 26:3-4; 28:13-14?
6. What about the promise in Genesis 15:18? "On that day the LORD made a covenant with Abram and said, 'To your descendants I give this land, from the river of Egypt to the great river, the Euphrates.'"

Going through Galatians

with Michael Penny

Study 8:
Galatians 3:19-25

The Law and The Promise:

Part 2

**Please read Galatians 3:15-18
and recap on the previous study
before starting this study.**

Galatians 3:19-25

1. What, then, was the purpose of the Law of Moses?

2. What does "It was added because of transgression until the Seed to whom the promise referred had come" mean?

3. Does the *NEB* translation of this phrase make it easier to understand? It has: "It was added to make wrongdoing a legal offence. It was a temporary measure pending the arrival of the 'issue' to whom the promise was made."

4. Note Paul's comments linking 'the law' and 'sin' in Romans: see 3:20; 4:15; 5:13; 5:20; 7:7; 7:13.

5. What role did angels play in the giving of the Law of Moses? (Deuteronomy 33:1-5)

6. Who was the 'mediator' between God and the people of Israel in the giving of the Law?

7. Look at the first covenant, the one associated with the Law of Moses: read Exodus 19:3-8. How many parties were involved in this first covenant?

8. Was the first covenant conditional or unconditional?

9. How many parties are involved in a promise (i.e. an unconditional covenant)?

10. Is a promise superior to the Law or to a conditional covenant?

11. Is the New Covenant of Jeremiah 31:31-34 a conditional covenant or a promise (i.e. an unconditional covenant)?

12. Is the Law opposed to the promises of God? If not,

why not? (See Romans 3:21;28-32)

13. Could God have given 'a' law which man could have kept and so man would have been able to gain righteousness and eternal life by observing that law?

14. If God had given such a law, what would it have said about God's character?

15. The whole world is a prisoner of sin! Do you agree? (See Ecclesiastes 7:20; Psalm 14:1-3; 53:1-3; Romans 3:10,23; Ephesians 2:1-6)

16. What was promised?

17. How was it given? (See also Ephesians 2:8-10.)

18. In what way were the Jews held prisoner by the Law?

19. How did the Law lead the Jews to Christ and to justification by faith?

20. If the Jews of the Acts period still had to obey the Law, what does Paul mean by "we are no longer under the 'supervision' of the law"? (Does Galatians 5:18 help, and the verses either side?)

Application

1. What is the purpose of our church's rules and regulations?
2. Are we under the New Covenant?
3. Were you a 'prisoner of sin'? Are you a 'prisoner of sin'?
4. We are not under the Law of Moses, but are we under the 'supervision' of some other law or code?

Going through Galatians

with Michael Penny

Study 9:
Galatians 3:26-4:7

Sons of God

Galatians 3:26-4:7

1. How do people become 'sons of God'? (Compare John 1:11-13; and John 3:3-7)

2. What does 'baptised into Christ mean? And how is this achieved? (Compare 1 Corinthians 10:1-5; Colossians 2:9-13)

3. What does Paul mean by 'you are all *one* in Christ Jesus' when, at that time, during the Acts period, there were significant differences between Jewish Christians and Gentiles Christians?

4. How did the Gentiles of that time become Abraham's seed?

5. What did it mean to be Abraham's seed? (Read Romans 4:12,16,23-25 and compare Romans 11:11-25)

Note: Galatians 3:26-29 was more pertinent to the Gentile Christians, but 4:1-7 was more relevant to the Jewish Christians.

6. Why is the child and heir (i.e. the Jews) no different from a slave?

7. What is symbolised by the 'guardians and trustees'? (Compare Galatians 3:23.)

8. What, to the Jews, were the 'basic principles of the world'? (Again compare 3:23)

9. When did the child and heir (the Jews) receive the 'full rights of sons'? And how was this achieved?

10. What was the result or consequences of this?

Application

1. What does your church teach on:
    - a) Baptism in water
    - b) identification
    - c) baptism in the Holy Spirit
    - d) filling by the Holy Spirit
2. Have you ever looked on yourself as 'the seed of Abraham'?
3. Should Christians, today, view themselves as 'the seed of Abraham'?

****

Note: An explanation of the terms in question 1 of the Application is given in chapters 8 and 9 of *The Miracles of the Apostles* by Michael Penny (published by The Open Bible Trust).

Details of this book can be seen on
www.obt.org.uk

It can be ordered from that website.

It is available as an eBook from Amazon and Apple and as a paperback from Amazon.

Going through Galatians

with Michael Penny

Study 10.

Galatians 4:8-20

Paul's Concern for the Gentile Christians in Galatia

Galatians 4:8-20

Note the use of 'we' in 4:3-5 and the reference to the Law of Moses in 4:5 – implying Paul was concerned with Jewish Christians.

1. Why does verse 8 imply Paul is now turning his concern to the Gentile Christians? (Compare Romans 1:21-23.) the similar phrase in the Jewish section
2. What are those 'weak and miserable principles' that Paul refers to in verse 9? (Contrast them to 'basic principles of the world', a similar phrase in the Jewish section; verse 3.)
3. How could the Gentiles be enslaved by these weak and miserable principles? (How were the Jews enslaved by the basic principles of the world?)
4. What special days and months and seasons and years did these Gentile Christians want to observe? Why were they wrong to do so? (What about the Jewish Christians of that time and their observation of certain days specified in the Law of Moses; were those Jewish Christians wrong to observe those days?)
5. In what way does Paul want them to become like him? In what way did he become like them?
6. What illness is Paul referring to in verses 13-16?
7. Was the illness something to do with the eyes? (See verse 15 and Galatians 6:11.)

8. When had Paul visited the Galatians and why had the illness been the reason that he had gone to Galatia?

Note Verses 17-20 really belong in the next section because Paul's next concern now turns to those Gentiles Christians who wish to be circumcised and observe the Law of Moses. These had been influenced by the Judaisers, Christians Jews who argued that the Gentiles had to be circumcised to be saved

9. Notice the personal concern has for the relationship he has with the Galatians; compare and contrast his comments in verse 16 with those in verse 20?
10. Why couldn't Paul visit the Galatians at this point in time? (Remember he wrote Galatians at the end of Acts 14 (verse 28) but note what was happening at Antioch at the time (Acts 15:1-2.)

Application

1. Are there any 'weak and miserable principles' today that Christians are inclined towards?
2. Are there any 'special days, months, seasons and years' Christians are inclined towards?
3. Should Jewish Christians today observe the days specified in the Law of Moses?
4. Are there any of the days specified in the Law of Moses that Gentile Christians should observe? (Note Acts 15:19-21 and 15:23-29 for Gentiles Christians during Acts, and Colossians 2:16-17 for ALL Christians after Acts – note also Colossians 2:13-14 and Ephesians 2:14-16 for the Mosaic Law in General.)

Going through Galatians

with Michael Penny

Study 11.
Galatians 4:21-31

Hagar and Sarah

Galatians 4:21-31

1. What do you know about Hagar? (Read Genesis chapters 16 & 21)
2. What do you know about Sarah? (Read Genesis chapters 15, 18 & 21)
3. What was the first (the Old) Covenant? (Read Exodus 19:1-6)
4. What were the conditions of this Old Covenant? (e.g. How many 'ifs'?)
5. What was the second (the New) Covenant? (Read Jeremiah 31:31-34)
6. What were the conditions of the New Covenant? (e.g. How many 'ifs'?)
7. Which covenant is based on law, obedience, works?
8. Which covenant is based on grace, faith?
9. Who were persecuting the Galatians Christians?
10. Does Paul actually tell the Galatians Christians to 'get rid of' the persecutors?

Application

1. We are not under the New Covenant (which was made with the House of Israel and the House of Judah – se Jeremiah 31:31-34) but its basis is grace and we, too, are under grace. Are there ways in which other Christians, who do not fully understand grace, persecute us, or argue against us?
2. How should we deal with such people?

Going through Galatians

with Michael Penny

Study 12.

Galatians 5:1-15

Freedom in Christ

Galatians 5:1-15

1. "It is for 'freedom' that Christ has set us free," Paul wrote. What did he mean by 'freedom' and what is the difference between 'freedom' and 'license'?
2. Why would Christ be of 'no value' if the Gentile Christians became circumcised?
3. Why would those Gentile Christians who became circumcised be obligated to keep the whole Law of Moses?
4. What does Paul mean when he states that those who are trying to be justified by the Law 'have been alienated from Christ' Doesn't Christ still love them?
5. What does 'fallen away from grace' mean? Does it mean that they have lost their salvation?
6. What 'righteousness' is Paul hoping for?
7. Is 'faith expressing itself in love' better than the Law? Stronger than the Law? More motivating than the Law?
8. Who was it that 'cut in' on the Galatians Gentiles Christians and inhibited their growth?
9. 'Yeast' in the Bible is symbol of sin, so to what was Paul referring when he wrote, 'A little yeast works through the whole batch of dough'?
10. Why was Paul confident the Gentile Christians in Galatia would do the right thing?
11. What penalty would the Judaisers (Jewish Christians who said that the Gentiles had to be circumcised to

be saved) pay? [Note: This penalty would be suffered 'no matter who they may be!]

12. When did Paul preach circumcision of the Gentiles? And when did he stop?

13. Verse12 is pretty strong; can you understand Paul's sentiments? (Remember when he wrote Galatians and the problems he was experiencing; see the end of Acts 14 and the start of Acts 15.)

14. Verse 13. See question 1 again: What is the difference between 'freedom' and 'license'?

15. Verse 14. See question 7 again: Is love strong than the Law? More motivating?

16. What should they not back-bite? Gossip? [Any ideas what this back-biting was about?]

Application

1. Are some churches / Christians today confusing 'freedom' and 'license'?
2. Is the 'permissiveness' of our society rubbing off on some Christians (especially the young perhaps – who need our prayers)?
3. What is the difference between 'permissiveness' and 'license'?
4. Is Christ made of 'no value' by certain rituals today in some part of Christendom?
5. If we follow certain rules in our church, are we 'obligated' to keep the whole lot?

Going through Galatians

with Michael Penny

Study 13.

Galatians 5:16-26

Life by the Spirit

Galatians 5:16-26

1. How do we avoid gratifying the desires of the sinful nature?
2. What are the desires of the sinful nature?
3. Each Christian has two natures; the sinful nature and the Holy Spirit dwelling inside. What is the result of this schizophrenia?
4. Read Romans 7:7-25. How long had Paul been a Christian when he wrote to the Roman about this problem?
5. How would you define each of the acts of the sinful nature?

Sexual immorality	
Impurity	
Debauchery	
Idolatry	
Witchcraft	
Hatred	
Discord	
Jealousy	
fits of rage	
selfish ambition	
Factions	
Envy	
Drunkenness	
Orgies	
and the like	

6. Why will people who 'live' like that not inherit the kingdom of God? (Compare 1 John 3:6 and not 1

John 1:8 – 2:2; see *KJV* version on 1 John 3:6 and
compare with *NIV.*)

7. How would you define each element of the fruit of
the Spirit?

Love	
Joy	
Peace	
Patience	
Kindness	
Goodness	
Faithfulness	
Gentleness	
Self-control	

8. How do we 'crucify' the sinful nature? (See
Colossians 3:1-17.)
9. How do we keep in step with the Spirit?
10. Why did Paul warn the Galatians against (a) being
conceited, (b) provoking each other, and (c) envying
each other?

Application

1. Which aspects of the sinful nature are the biggest problems for Christians today?
2. Which aspects of the fruit of the Spirit do Christians today struggle with most?

Going through Galatians

with Michael Penny

Study 14.

Galatians 6:1-10

Doing good

Galatians 6:1-10

1. What does it mean to be 'caught' in a sin? After all, we all sin and 1 John 1:10 states: "If we claim we have not sinned, we make him out to be a liar and his word has no place in our lives."
2. For verse 1, the *New English Bible* has, "If a man should do something wrong, my brothers, on a sudden impulse." Is this better / clearer?
3. Young's *Literal Translation* has "if a man be overtaken in a trespass": has that more meaning?
4. Compare this verse in Galatians with 1 John 3:6:
(a) "Whosoever abideth in him sinneth not: whosoever sinneth hath not seen him, neither known him." (*KJV*)
(b) "No one who lives in him keeps on sinning. No one who continues to sin has either seen him or known him." (*NIV*)
5. What does it mean to 'restore' the person?
(a) *The Living Bible* has: "help him back onto the right path";
(b) *The Amplified Bible* has: "set him right and restore and reinstate him, without any sense of superiority and with all gentleness."
6. How should that 'restoration' be done?
7. Why should it be done in that way?
8. What is the difference between a burden – "carry each other's burdens" (v 2) – and a load – "each one should carry his own load" (v 5)?

(a) 'burden' is *baros* and refers to pressures or weights, maybe of society, which can pressurise a person to be overtaken in a sin.

(b) 'load' is *phortion* and is used of a soldier's back pack, and refers to the individual responsibilities a person has (e.g. 1 Timothy 5:8).

9. How can a person deceive himself? (Compare Ephesians 4:1-2 and especially Philippians 2:1-4.)

10. To which person should we compare ourselves?

11. Why should we do good?

12. To whom should we do good? And who has first call on the good we do?

Application

1. How do Christians, who are 'caught' in a sin, respond / react to being 'set right'?
2. Colossians 3:16 has, "Let the word of Christ dwell in you richly as you teach and admonish one another with all wisdom." How do Christians today respond / react to being 'admonished'?
3. How would you like to be 'put right' and be 'admonished'?
4. Would you / could you, 'put right' or 'admonish' another Christian?
5. What are the burdens / pressures in today's society which cause Christians to be overtaken by a sin?
6. What are the individual loads Christians should carry in today's society? (That is, ones for which they should not expect help from other Christians – but what about help from the State?)
7. Can a person who sows to his 'sinful nature' be a Christian? (Remember 1 John 3:6 above.)
8. Have we ever grown weary of doing good?

Going through Galatians

with Michael Penny

Study 15.

Galatians 6:11-18

Not circumcision
But
A New Creation

Galatians 6:11-18

1. The build of Paul's letters were dictated and written by an amanuensis. Did Paul write the end parts of other letters? (See Romans 16:22; 1 Corinthians 16:21; Colossians 4:18; 2 Thessalonians 3:17. Note 2 Thessalonians 2:2; Paul's 'grace signature' in each of his letters may well have been written in his own hand.)
2. Why did the Judaisers want to circumcise the Gentile Christians?
3. Who did the Judaisers want to impress?
4. Whose persecution did the Judaisers want to avoid?
5. What did the Judaisers want to boast about?
6. Who did Paul want to boast about? (See also 1 Corinthians 1:31.)
7. How was the world 'crucified' to Paul, and how was he 'crucified' to the world?
8. Why doesn't it matter whether a person is circumcised or not?
9. 'Peace' and 'mercy': what does 'peace' mean and what does 'mercy' mean?
10. Paul asks for 'peace and mercy' …. "**even on** the Israel of God". This is the only occurrence of this term 'the Israel of God' in the Scripture; to whom does it refer? (Note the 'even on'.)
11. Why doesn't Paul want anyone to cause him trouble?

12. To what is Paul referring when he speaks of bearing 'the marks of Jesus' on his body? (Remember Acts 14:19 and see 2 Corinthians 6:4-6; 2 Corinthians 11:4-5.)

Application

1. Is there a temptation today for some Christians to want to curry favour with certain people and to avoid persecution?
2. Who are they tempted to curry favour from?
3. What persecution do they wish to avoid?
4. "Neither circumcision nor uncircumcision means anything; what counts is a new creation." What words could we substitute for 'circumcision'?
5. Is the world 'crucified' to us, and are we 'crucified' to the world?

Going through Galatians

with Michael Penny

Study 16.

Galatians

Conclusion

Conclusion

Three important things I hope we have learnt are:

1. The gospel of salvation by grace through faith is of paramount importance and must never be compromised, not even in the slightest.
2. That we need to look at the Bible historically first, putting it and its teaching in its natural setting. Only after that should we seek to apply it to ourselves and our society.
3. Galatians, like most / all of Paul letters, deals with doctrinal issues first before dealing with practical matters. This is the principle of doctrine before practice.

Post Script

It is sincerely hoped that readers have enjoyed this series on Galatians. It may have been hard going at times, but having finished Galatians you may now wish to go back and read right through Galatians in one sitting. Those who have done this have been surprised by how much they have learnt and remembered.

However, you may also wish to read a book on Galatians and you may like to read *Galatians: Interpretation and Application* by Michael Penny. This book puts the historical setting (the interpretation) first, but then considers applications to the 21st Century.

This is available as an eBook from either Amazon (for Kindles and Androids) or from Apple (for iPads etc.).

It is also available as a KDP Paperback from Amazon.

****

Other Study Guides

A Study Guide to
Psalm 119
By Michael Penny

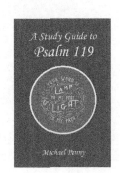

A very useful guide to Psalm 119 indicating …

- It is the longest Psalm;
- It is an Acrostic Psalm – and gives an acrostic translation of the first 24 verses;
- The Ten Hebrews words which recur throughout the Psalm.

Each group of eight verses is considered separately – giving 22 studies.

Each group is given in two translation presented in parallel for ease of comparison.

For each group a task is set for personals study or group discussion.

And at the end of each group, as a conclusion, there is page or so of commentary.

Manual on the Gospel of John

By Michael Penny

"If you are stuck for an idea with your group,
try The Manual on the Gospel of John."
(Eric Thorn, reviewed in *The Connexion*)

This book was produced with college students for college students, but is valuable for any age range. It asks and answers the questions the students asked about John's Gospel, but in a novel way.

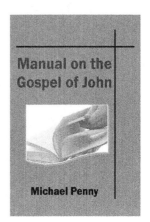

The book is in four parts:

1) Aims of the Book; How to use the Book
2) Questions with Aids and Hints to the Answers
3) Questions with Answers and Further Information
4) Main themes of John's Gospel

This book is ideal for not only for personal study, but also for Youth Groups, House Groups, and Bible Study Groups. The questions in Section Two can be discussed and answered, and there and Aids and Hints to help. After being discussed and answered, the author's answers and comments can be reviewed from Section Three.

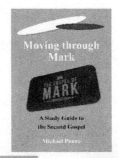
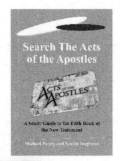

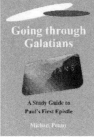
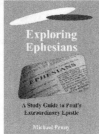

Learning from Luke

A Study Guide to the Gospel sent to a Gentile

Moving through Mark

A Study Guide to the Second Gospel

Search the Acts of the Apostles

A Study Guide to the

Fifth Book of the New Testament

Going through Galatians

A Study Guide to Paul's First Letter

Exploring Ephesians

A Study Guide to Paul's Extraordinary Epistle

Further details of all the books on these pages
can be seen on

www.obt.org.uk

The books are available from that website and from

The Open Bible Trust
Fordland Mount, Upper Basildon,
Reading, RG8 8LU, UK.

They are also available as eBooks from Amazon and
Apple and as
KDP paperback from Amazon

About the author

Michael Penny was born in Ebbw Vale, Gwent, Wales in 1943. He read Mathematics at the University of Reading, before teaching for twelve years and becoming the Director of Mathematics and Business Studies at Queen Mary's College Basingstoke in Hampshire, England. In 1978 he entered Christian publishing, and in 1984 became the administrator of The Open Bible Trust.

He held this position for seven years, before moving to the USA and becoming pastor of Grace Church in New Berlin, Wisconsin. He returned to Britain in 1999, and is at present the Administrator and Editor of The Open Bible Trust. From 2010 he has been Chair of Churches Together in Reading, and from 2019 Chair of Churches Together in Berkshire, where he speaks in a number of churches of different denominations. In 2019. He is also a member of the Advisory Committee to Reading

University Christian Union and a chaplain at Reading College.

He is lead chaplain for Activate Learning Colleges and has set up chaplaincy teams in a number of their colleges including Reading College, The City of Oxford College, Bracknell and Wokingham College, and Blackbird Leys College, and is at present looking at Guildford College and Banbury College.

He lives near Reading with his wife and has appeared on Premier Radio man times and is frequently on BBC Radio.

He has made several speaking tours of America, Canada, Australia, New Zealand and the Netherlands, as well as others to South Africa and the Philippines. Some of his writings have been translated into German and Russian.

In 2019 the Bishop of Reading nominated him to receive Maundy Money from the Queen.

Also by Michael Penny

He has written many books including:

40 Problem Passages,
Galatians: Interpretation and Application,
Joel's Prophecy: Past and Future,
Approaching the Bible,
The Miracles of the Apostles,
The Manual on the Gospel of John
The Bible! Myth or Message?
Comments and Queries about the New Testament
Comments and Queries about Christianity

Also

The Will of God: Past and Present (with W M Henry)
Following Philippians (with W M Henry)
Abraham and his seed (with W M Henry & Sylvia Penny)
Introducing God's Plan (with Sylvia Penny)
Introducing God's Word (with Carol Brown & Lynn Mrotek)

His latest four books are:

James: His life and letter
Peter: His life and letters.
Paul: A Missionary of Genius
John: His life, death and writings

Approaching the Bible
By Michael Penny

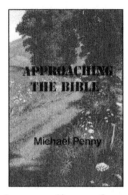

To gain a better understanding of any book of the Bible, including the Gospel of Luke, it is important to set it in the context of the other books. This is just what Michael Penny does in *Approaching the Bible*. Each book of the Bible is seen in relation to each other to gain an overall, and greater, appreciation of what the Scriptures teach about the plan and purposes of almighty God.

Reviews:
What other have said about *Approaching the Bible*!

Paul C. Clark, pastor, Great Kills Bible Chapel, Staten Island, NY; *Librarian's World*, official publication of Evangelical Church Library Association.

This is a thoroughgoing exposition and defense of the dispensationalist approach to interpreting the Bible. The author traces what he believes to be such an approach from some of the earliest Church Fathers onwards, points out the strengths and weaknesses in the dispensational system of modern interpreters, and advocates what he holds to be an improved approach. He sees Acts 28:28 as the watershed between God's dealings with Jews and Gentiles.

Frank Wren, *Trumpet Sounds*

A good book for those who want to study seriously the Word of God. It delves into basic areas to lay a good foundation for understanding the message using certain guidelines set by Miles Coverdale.

Charles Ozanne, *Search*

A book of sterling quality, simple and lucid but at the same time comprehensive and profound. Michael Penny does not assume that his readers already have a knowledge of the Bible in any detail. He starts from the very beginning and leads his readers by simple stages. No one who reads these pages can fail to be enlightened and to be clearer in his thinking as a result.

The Miracles of the Apostles

Michael Penny

Why did the Apostles perform miracles?
Why were they able to perform them?
What was the purpose of the miracles?
What did they signify to the Jews?
Why did the Gentiles misunderstand them?
Why was Paul, later, not able to heal?
When did the miracles cease?
Why did they cease?

This book answers these questions, explains the significance and purpose of each type of miracle performed by the Apostles, and makes it clear why such miracles are not in evidence today.

Search magazine

Michael Penny is editor of *Search* magazine.

For a free sample of
the Open Bible Trust's magazine *Search*, please email

admin@obt.org.uk

or visit

www.obt.org.uk/search

Publications of The Open Bible Trust must be in accordance with its evangelical, fundamental and dispensational basis. However, beyond this minimum, writers are free to express whatever beliefs they may have as their own understanding, provided that the aim in so doing is to further the object of The Open Bible Trust. A copy of the doctrinal basis is available on **www.obt.org.uk** or from:

THE OPEN BIBLE TRUST
Fordland Mount, Upper Basildon,
Reading, RG8 8LU, UK

Printed in Great Britain
by Amazon

19999154R00068